Return to O

Composed by coba

株式会社 現代ギター社
GG619

GENDAI GUITAR CO., LTD.
1-16-14 Chihaya, Toshima-ku, Tokyo, Japan

●緒言

Return to O （リターン・トゥ・オー）

2016年のデュオ作品に引き続き、再び荘村清志さんから Hakuju ギター・フェスタのための委嘱作品の依頼を受けました。しかも 2017 年はギターソロを、とのこと。

どんな曲にしようかと思い悩んでいた時に、ふと脳裏に浮かんだのが、19歳の時に留学2年目のイタリアで出会って大きな衝撃を受けた曲、フェリーチェ・フガッツァ作曲の〈Sonatina〉でした。それまでのクラシックアコーディオンのオリジナル曲といえば、調性感が全く無い現代音楽風の作品がほとんどでした。その中にあってこの曲は、豊かな音楽性を持って調性と無調性の間をハイセンスに行き来しながらストーリー展開する斬新なものでした。それまでに知っていたどの作品とも一線を劃すこの曲に出会ったことで、その後の自身の活動に大きな方向性を授けられた気がします。

そんなギター作品を書けたら、という僕の思いが〈Return to O〉には集約されています。ギターの持つ荒々しいグルーヴと幽玄の鳴りがこの〈Return to O〉で実現出来たら素敵だと思う次第です。

O は Own であり Only であり Original であり Zero（零）であります。

coba

● Preface

Return to O

Following the duo work written in 2016, I received another commission from Mr. Kiyoshi Shomura for the Hakuju Guitar Festival. Only this time in 2017, it was for a solo guitar piece!

When I thought of what style to write in, a work I discovered during the second year of my studies in Italy, at the age of 19, crossed my mind : 'Sonatina' by Felice Fugazza. Previously, most original music for the classical accordion was written in atonal, avant-garde language. Amongst such works, the Sonatina is an innovative work, stylishly moving between tonality and atonality with imaginative musicality as the story of the piece develops. When I met this work which makes a clear distinction to other works I knew, I was imparted with clear direction for my musical activity which followed.

'Return to O' integrates my desire to write such a work for the guitar. It would be wonderful if both the harsh groove and subtlety inherent to the guitar would be realized in 'Return to O'.

O refers to Own, Only, Original and the number 0 (zero).

coba

●作品データ／ Works

第 12 回 Hakuju ギター・フェスタ 2017 委嘱作品。
2017 年 8 月 18 日、荘村清志により、Hakuju Hall（東京）にて初演。

This work was written for the '12th Hakuju Guitar Festival 2017'.
Premiered on August 8, 2017 by Kiyoshi Shomura, at the Hakuju Hall in Tokyo.

● coba
（アコーディオニスト・作曲家／ Accordionist, Composer）

18歳でイタリアに留学、ヴェネツィアのルチアーノ・ファンチェル音楽院アコーディオン科を首席卒業。在学中1980年世界アコーディオンコンクールで東洋人として初優勝。以来ヨーロッパ各国でのCDリリース、チャート第1位獲得など、"coba"の名前と音楽は国境を越え世界の音楽シーンに影響を与え続けている。

常にアコーディオンの限界に挑戦しながら、斬新なサウンドを追及した作品は、内外に高い評価を得る。作曲家としての活躍も多岐に渡り、現在までのテレビ、映画、舞台、CM音楽作品は500作を越える。楽曲提供も各オーケストラ、荘村清志、舘野 泉、十亀正司、沢田研二、藤井フミヤ等多岐に渡る。

日本レコード大賞特別賞、日本アカデミー賞音楽優秀賞を受賞。2017年アコーディオンの聖地、イタリア・カステルフィダルド市にて名誉市民賞を受賞。

He moved to Italy at the age of 18, where he studied accordion at Scuola di musica Luciano Fancelli in Venice, graduating as the top student. During his studies, he was awarded first prize at the 1980 Trophée Mondiale de l'Accordéon as the first Asian winner. He has subsequently released CDs throughout Europe, achieving Chart no.1. The name "coba" and his music crosses borders and is a major influence in the world musical scene.

His works, constantly pushing the possibilities of the accordion and pursuing novel sonorities, are regarded highly both in and out of Japan. As a composer, he has written a wide range of more than 500 works for television, movies, stage and commercials. He has written commissioned works for many orchestras, as well as for such artists as Kiyoshi Shomura, Izumi Tateno, Masashi Togame, Kenji Sawada and Fumiya Fujii.

He has received Special Prize at Japan Record Award and 'Outstanding Achievement in Music' at Japan Academy Prize. In 2017, he was made honorary citizen of Castelfidardo, Italy, the accordion capital of the world.

Return to O

Fingered by Kiyoshi Shomura

coba
(2017/2018)

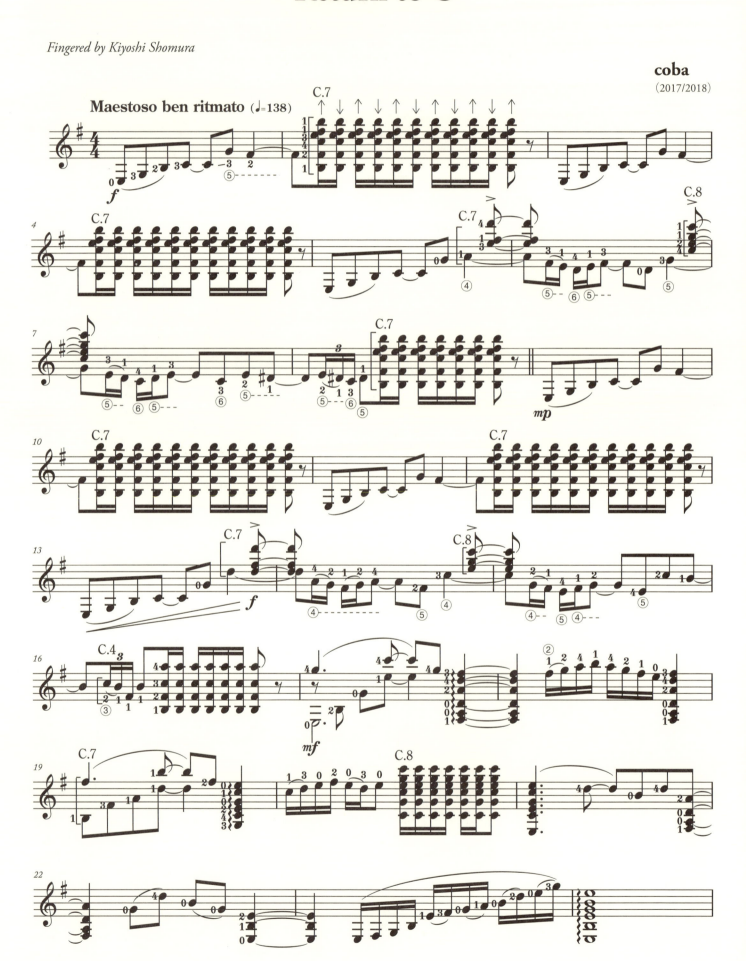

Return to O Composed by coba 定価 ［本体 2,000 円 + 税］ GG619	2018年9月10日初版発行 発行元 ● 株式会社 現代ギター社 〒171-0044 東京都豊島区千早1-16-14 TEL03-3530-5423　FAX03-3530-5405 無断転載を禁ず　日本音楽著作権協会（出）許諾第1809240-801号 印刷・製本 ● シナノ印刷 株式会社 表紙 ● 株式会社現代ギター社 楽譜浄書 ● ウッドノート・スタジオ コード番号 ● ISBN 978-4-87471-619-9　C3073　¥2000E © coba Gendai Guitar Co., Ltd. 1-16-14 Chihaya, Toshima-ku, Tokyo 171-0044, JAPAN　http://www.gendaiguitar.com 1st edition : September 10th, 2018　Printed in Japan

楽譜や歌詞・音楽書などの出版物を権利者に無断で複製（コピー）することは、著作権の侵害（私的利用など特別な場合を除く）にあたり、著作権法により罰せられます。
また、出版物からの不法なコピーが行なわれますと、出版社は正常な出版活動が困難となり、ついには皆様方が必要とされるものも出版できなくなります。
音楽出版社と日本音楽著作権協会（JASRAC）は、著作者の権利を守り、なおいっそう優れた作品の出版普及に全力をあげて努力してまいります。どうか不法コピーの防止に、皆様方のご協力をお願い申し上げます。

（株）現代ギター社
（社）日本音楽著作権協会